GW00419451

Fourteen solid gold standards.

FRANK SINATRA · GOLD CLASSICS

Wise Publications.

LONDON / NEW YORK / SYDNEY

Exclusive distributors:
Music Sales Limited
8/9 Frith Street, London W1V 5TZ, England.
Music Sales Pty Limited
120 Rothschild Avenue, Rosebery, NSW 2018, Australia.

This book © Copyright 1989 by Wise Publications
UK ISBN 0.7119.1845.7
Order No. AM. 74949

Designed by Pearce Marchbank Studio

Compiled by Peter Evans

MY WAY

WORDS BY PAUL ANKA · MUSIC BY CLAUDE FRANCOIS & JACQUES REVAUX

all _____ when there was doubt _____ I ate it up _____ and spit it
things _____ he'd tru - ly feel _____ and not the words _____ of one who

out. _____ I faced it all _____ and I stood tall _____ and did it
kneels. The re - cord shows _____ I took the

my way. _____ I've

D.%. al Coda

CODA

blows _____ and did it my way.

rit. _____ ff

Oh Look At Me Now

WORDS BY JOHN DEVRIES · MUSIC BY JOE BUSHKIN

8

brand new start, ___ I'm so proud I'm bust-in' my vest. ___
Gon-na be Mis - iz, not Miss. ___ So,

I am the guy ___ (girl) ___ who turned out a lov - er, So, I'm the guy, ___ (girl) ___ who

laughed at those blue ___ dia - mond rings, ___ one of those things, ___

___ Oh! Look At Me Now. ___ Now. ___

The Lady Is A Tramp

WORDS BY LORENZ HART · MUSIC BY RICHARD RODGERS

It's Nice To Go Trav'ling

WORDS BY SAMMY CAHN · MUSIC BY JAMES VAN HEUSEN

oh, so nice_ to wan-der back!
1. The mam-'selles and frau - lein_ and the
2. You will find the maed - chen_ and the

se - ño - ri - tas are sweet,
gay mu - cha - chas are rare,
But they can't com-pete, 'cause they just don't
But they can't com-pare with the sex - y

have What the mod - els have _____ on Mad - i - son Ave.
line That pa - rades each day _____ at Sun - set and Vine.

It's ver - y nice _____ to be foot-loose With just a tooth-brush and
It's quite the life _____ to play gyp - sy And roam as gyp - sies will

13

trav-'ling, But it's, oh, so___ nice_____ to come home!   2. It's ver - y

trav-'ling, But it's, oh, so___ nice_

___ to come home!

to come home!   No more cus - toms!

Burn the pass - port!   No more pack - ing!

And un - pack - ing!   Light the home - fires!

Get my slip - pers!   Start a piz - za!

15

I'LL NEVER SMILE AGAIN, UNTIL I SMILE AT YOU

WORDS & MUSIC BY RUTH LOWE

COME FLY WITH ME

LYRICS BY SAMMY CAHN · MUSIC BY JIMMY VAN HEUSEN

COME FLY WITH ME! Let's fly! Let's fly a-way!

If you can use some ex-ot-ic booze there's a bar in far Bom-
(views)

bay, COME FLY WITH ME! Let's fly! Let's fly a-way!

COME FLY WITH ME! Let's float down to Pe-ru! In

EAST OF THE SUN (AND WEST OF THE MOON)

WORDS & MUSIC BY BROOKS BOWMAN

you and I._____ East of the sun_____ and

west of the moon,_____ We'll build a dream-house___ of

love, dear. Near to the sun in the

day, Near to the moon at night, We'll

23

live in a love-ly way, dear, Liv-ing on love and pale moon-light.

Just you and I,_____ for ev-er and a day,_____

_____ Love will not die,_____ we'll

keep it that way,_____ Up a-mong the

ANGEL EYES

WORDS BY EARL BRENT · MUSIC BY MATT DENNIS

An-gel eyes_ that old dev-il sent_ they glow un-bear-a-bly bright_

Need I say_ that my love's mis-spent,_ mis-spent with an-gel eyes to-night._

So drink up,_____ all you peo - ple,_ Or-der an-y-thing you see,_

Have fun,_____ you hap-py peo-ple,_ The drink and the laugh's_ on me._

Par-don me,___ but I "got-ta run"___

The fact's un-com-mon-ly clear,___ Got-ta find___ who's

now "num-ber one"___ and why my an-gel eyes ain't here.___

'Scuse me while I dis-ap-pear.___

STRANGERS IN THE NIGHT

WORDS BY CHARLES SINGLETON & EDDIE SNYDER · MUSIC BY BERT KAEMPFERT

warm em-bracing dance a-way and ev-er since that night_____ we've been to-geth-er,

Lov-ers at first sight,_____ In love for-ev-er, It turned out so right,_____

_____ For strangers in the night._____

night._____

The Very Thought Of You

WORDS & MUSIC BY RAY NOBLE

For sleep-ing or wak-ing, dear,__ I find;__
I'll on-ly be sat-is-fied__ with you;__

REFRAIN

The ver-y thought of you,_____ And I for-get to do,__

The lit-tle or-di-na-ry things that ev'ry-one

ought to do._____ I'm liv-ing in a kind of

33

day - dream, I'm hap - py as a king, And fool - ish tho' it

may seem, To me_____ that's ev' - ry - thing._____ The mere i -

dea of you,_____ The long - ing here for you,_____

You'll nev - er know how slow the mo - ments go 'till I'm

The Night We Called It A Day

WORDS BY TOM ADAIR · MUSIC BY MATT DENNIS

CHORUS

IF I HAD YOU

WORDS & MUSIC BY TED SHAPIRO, JIMMY CAMPBELL & REG CONNELLY

SOMETHIN' STUPID

WORDS & MUSIC BY C. CARSON PARKS

Moderately slow

mf
F F6 Fmaj7 F
mp
I know I stand in line un-til you think you have the time to spend an
prac-tice ev-'ry day to find some cle-ver lines to say to make the
Gm7 C9 Gm7 C9 Gm7 C7
eve-nin' with me. And if we go some place to dance, I
mean-ing come through. But then I think I'll wait un-til the
Gm7 C7 Fmaj7 F6
know that there's a chance you won't be leav-in' with me.
eve-nin' gets late and I'm a-lone with you.

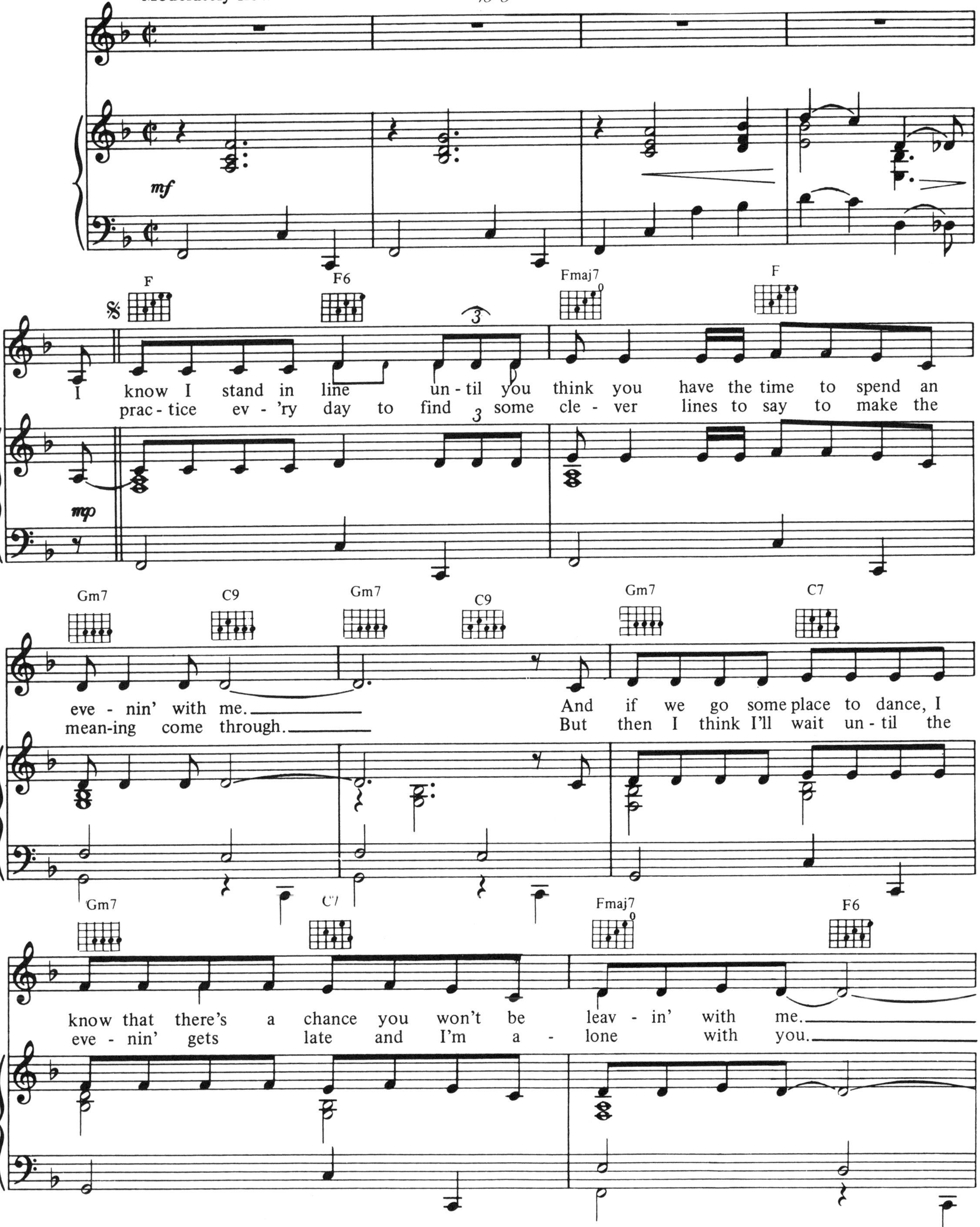

I've Got You Under My Skin

WORDS & MUSIC BY COLE PORTER